J. F. (John Freckleton) Burrowes, W. C. (William Cumming) Peters

Burrowes' Piano-forte Primer

J. F. (John Freckleton) Burrowes, W. C. (William Cumming) Peters

Burrowes' Piano-forte Primer

ISBN/EAN: 9783744793506

Printed in Europe, USA, Canada, Australia, Japan

Cover: Foto ©Thomas Meinert / pixelio.de

More available books at **www.hansebooks.com**

BURROWES'

PIANO-FORTE

PRIMER,

CONTAINING THE

RUDIMENTS OF MUSIC,

CALCULATED

EITHER FOR PRIVATE TUITION,

OR,

TEACHING IN CLASSES.

REVISED AND ENLARGED, WITH ADDITIONS
AND ALTERATIONS,

BY W. C. PETERS.

RICHMOND, VA:
J. W. RANDOLPH, PUBLISHER.
1864.

PREFACE.

THE rapid sale of this little work, and the flattering approbation which has been bestowed upon it by many of the most eminent Professors, have given great satisfaction to the Author. In presenting another edition to the musical world, he begs to repeat, that it is not intended to interfere with the mode of instruction which any Master has already adopted, but to be used either in private tuition or teaching in classes, in *addition* to the regular lessons already in use.

The author thinks it necessary to repeat, that he does not offer this book as containing anything *new;* yet he hopes it will be found useful in explaining the rudiments, and thereby enabling the Master to devote more time to other important branches of music.

The following remarks, although certainly superfluous to professors in general, he hopes will not be thought intrusive.

The principal object of every teacher should be, to make his pupils thoroughly comprehend one question, before they proceed to another; for this purpose each one should be provided with a music slate, upon which, after explanation, the teacher should write an exercise drawn from the questions or the Appendix, leaving the blanks to be filled up by the pupils.

Every exercise should be repeated, and the form of it varied, until it be done without a mistake, and until the pupil be able to give an Example upon the instrument, or answer any question, whether proposed in the regular order or otherwise. This will be attended with a little trouble to the Master in the first instance only, as the author recommends that the *learners* of the *second* chapter, should be *teachers* of the *first;* and this should be done at a distant part of the room in which the Master is giving his lessons at the piano-forte, that he may, by way of keeping up the attention of the scholars, occasionally inspect their Examples; and it is recommended that an examination of the whole school should take place at stated periods.

Pupils of talent to be removed to the upper classes as soon as the Master finds them qualified, without waiting for those who are less rapid in their improvement.

The Exercise of each class to be appointed by the Master. They may be selected either from the Primer, or by making the pupils explain to the teacher the lesson about to be played; both the time marked and manner of counting it throughout, pointing out those Notes from which the fingers are to be raised, those Notes which are to be held down, the reasons for the fingering, &c;, &c.

The classes to be held only during the time the Master is giving his lessons at the piano-forte.

The younger pupils to be attended at their daily practice by one of the elder ones, who is to be appointed by the Master.

After being made thoroughly acquainted with the contents of this book, the pupils may proceed to the study of Harmony, and the practice of playing from figured bases.

THE

PIANO-FORTE PRIMER.

CHAPTER I.

OF THE KEYS, STAFF, ETC.

How are the Keys of the Piano Forte named?

From the first seven letters of the alphabet: the Eighth, or Octave, is a repetition of the first. Example: A, B, C, D, E, F, G, A, B, C, D, E, &c.

How are the Letters applied to the Keys?

First, by observing that the Black Keys are divided into groups of two and three. D, is between the *two* Black Keys; G, is on the left, and A, on the right, between the *three* Black ones.

Describe the situation of the others.

C, is on the left; and E, on the right hand side of D. F, is on the left of G; and B, on the right of A.

What is a Staff?

A Staff consists of five Lines and four Spaces, upon which the Notes are placed, and named regularly by degrees.

The five Lines and four Spaces make nine Degrees. If you wish more Degrees, how are they formed?

By using the Space above or below the Staff, or by making short lines, called Added or Ledger Lines, on which, or the Spaces between or above them, the notes are placed.

3rd Ledger Space above the Staff

2nd Ledger Line above. ——

2nd Ledger Space above the Staff.

1st Ledger Line above. ——

1st Ledger Space above the Staff.

5th Line.——————————————9——

8 4th Space

4th Line.—————————————7————

6 3rd Space.

3rd Line.——————————5————

4 2nd Space.

2nd Line.——————————3————

2 1st Space.

1st Line.————1————————

1st Ledger Space below the Staff.

1st Ledger Line below. ——

2nd Ledger Space below the Staff.

2nd Ledger Line below. ——

3rd Ledger Space below the Staff.

How many Staffs are in general use?

Two. The Treble and the Base Staff.

How are you to know the Treble Staff from the Base Staff?

By the character placed at the beginning of each Staff. called a Clef, or Key to the names of the Notes.

What Clef is generally used for the Treble, or right hand?

The G, or Treble Clef, viz. 

What Clef is generally used for the Base or left hand?

The F, or Base Clef, viz: 

In Piano-Forte music the two Staffs are joined together by what is called a Brace, thus—

Why is the Treble Clef Note called G?

Because the Note placed on the second Line in the Treble is called G, or the Treble Clef Note.

How are the names of the other Treble Notes named?

They are named from the Clef Note, proceeding regularly by degrees, both upwards and downwards.

As the Note on the second Line in the Treble is called G, what will be the name of a Note in the second Space?

If the Note on the second Line in the Treble is called G, the second Space will be the next letter, which is A; the third Line B; the third Space C, &c.

Name the Treble Notes in the Staff, upwards and downwards; point out the Clef Note.

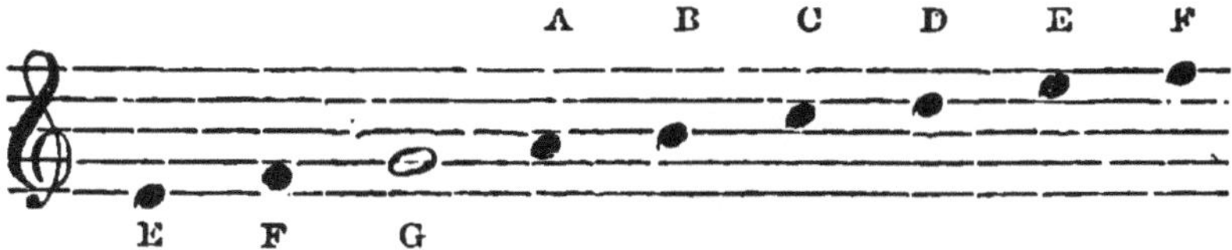

Why is the Base Clef Note called F?

Because the Note placed on the fourth Line in the Base is called F, or the Base Clef Note.

How are the names of the other Notes determined?

In the same manner as the Treble Notes, viz., from the Clef Note, both upwards and downwards.

As the Note on the fourth Line in the Base is called F, what will be the name of a Note in the fourth Space?

If the Note on the fourth Line in the Base is called F, the fourth Space will be the next letter, which is G, the fifth Line, A; above the Staff, B, &c.

Name the Base Notes in the Staff, upwards and downwards.

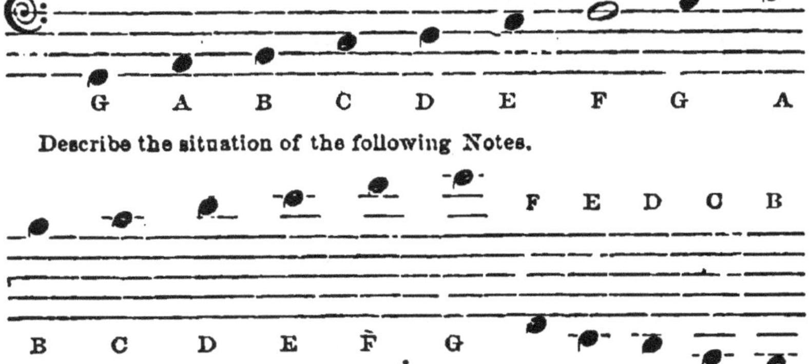

Describe the situation of the following Notes.

The Pupil should give a clear description, and tell the name of each note in the Treble and Base Clefs.

Name the Treble Notes, upwards and downwards, beginning with the Clef Note.

Name the Base Notes, upwards and downwards, beginning with the Clef Note,

How do you determine the situation of the Clef Notes on the Piano Forte?

First, by finding the C, which is nearest to the middle of the instrument, called middle C: the G, or Treble Clef Note, is the first G, above, or on the right hand side of it: the F, or Base Clef Note, is the first F, below, or on the left hand side of middle C.

How are the situations of the other Notes determined?

By going to the right, for those above; and to the left, for those below the Clef Notes.

Give an exercise for naming and striking some Treble and Base Notes.

CHAPTER 11.

OF THE LENGTH OF NOTES, RESTS, ETC.

How many different sorts of Notes are in general use?

Six.

Describe and show their different forms.

Semibreve. Minim. Crotchet. Quaver. Semiquaver. Demisemiquaver.

What proportion do they bear to each other?

Each note is only half the length of the one preceding; for example, a Minim is only half the length of a Semibreve, consequently one Semibreve is as long as two Minims.

Suppose you should wish to know how many Semiquavers are equal to a Semibreve or Minim, in what manner will you reckon them?

By beginning from any one, and proceeding in rotation, always doubling the number; for example, one Crochet is as long as two Quavers, four Semiquavers, or eight Demisemiquavers.

Repeat the general Table of the value of Notes.

Semibreve.		Minims.		Crotchets.		Quavers.		Semiquavers.		Demisemiquavers.
	=	2	=	4	=	8	=	16	=	32
			=	2	=	4	=	8	=	16
					=	2	=	4	=	8
							=	2	=	4
									=	2

Name the half, the fourth, the eighth, the sixteenth of a Semibreve; of a Minim, Crotchet, Quaver, &c.

What are Rests?

Marks for silence, corresponding with the different Notes.

Describe and show them.

Semibreve Rest.	*Minim Rest.*	*Crotchet Rest.*	*Quaver Rest.*	*Semiquaver Rest.*	*Demisemiq'r Rest.*
Under a Line.	Over a Line.	Turned to the right.	Turned to the left.	With two Heads.	With three Heads.

What is the use of a Dot after any Note or Rest?

A Dot is equal to half the preceding Note; consequently a Semibreve with a Dot, is equal to three Minims, or six Crochets, &c. A Dotted Crochet is as long as three Quavers, &c.

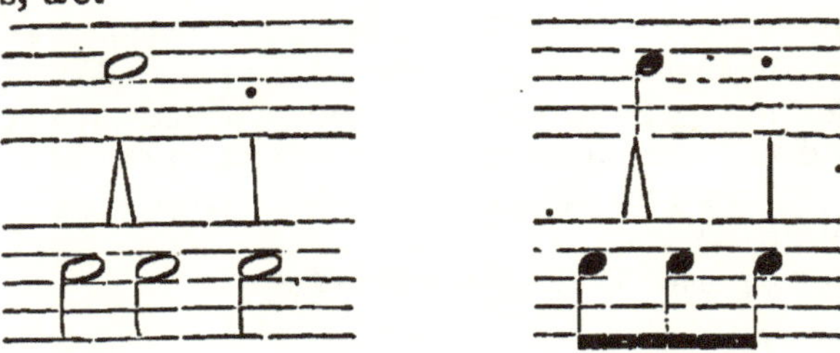

What is a Triplet?

When *three* Quavers, instead of *two*, are played to a Crochet,, they are called a Triplet; or three Semiquavers, instead of two, to a Quaver; and in the same proportion to all the other notes. Triplets are generally, but not always, marked with a figure of 3.

A figure of 6 is sometimes placed over six Quavers or Semiquavers, &c. What does it signify?

It signifies that the six Quavers are to be played in the time of four, or in the time of one Minim.

F NOTES, RESTS, ETC., NEWLY EXPLAINED.

How many different kinds of Notes are in general use?

Six.

Describe and show their different forms.

A Whole Note has a shape like an O, thus

A Half Note is shaped like a whole note, with a stem turned up or down, thus,

A Quarter Note has a black head, with a stem, thus,

An Eighth Note has a black head, with a stem and *one* hook, thus,

A Sixteenth Note has a black head, with a stem and two hooks, thus,

A Thirty-second Note has a black head, with a stem and *three* hooks, thus,

What proportion do the several Notes bear to each other?

Each Note is only half the length of the one preceding; for example, a Half Note is only half as long as a Whole Note, consequently a Whole Note is as long as two Half Notes.

Suppose you wish to know how many Sixteenth Notes are equal to a Whole Note, or Half Note, in what manner would you reckon them?

By beginning from any one, and proceeding in rotation, always doubling the number; for example, one Quarter Note is equal to two Eights, four Sixteenths, or eight Thirty-second Notes.

Repeat the general Table of the value of Notes.

Whole Note.		Half Notes.		Quarter Notes.		Eighth Notes.		Sixteenth Notes.		Thirty-second Notes.
𝅝	=	2	=	4	=	8	=	16	=	32
		𝅗𝅥	=	2	=	4	=	8	=	16
				♩	=	2	=	4	=	8
						♪	=	2	=	4
								𝅘𝅥𝅯	=	2
										𝅘𝅥𝅰

Name the half, the fourth, the eighths, the sixteenths, &c., of a Whole Note, of a Half Note, of a Fourth Note, of a Sixteenth Note, &c.

What are Rests?

Marks for silence, corresponding with the different Notes.

Describe and show them.

Whole Note Rest.	Half Note Rest.	Quarter Note Rest.	Eighth Note Rest.	Sixteenth Note Rest.	Thirty-second Rest.

Block under a Line.	Block over a Line.	Stem with a hook to the right.	Stem with a hook to the left.	Stem, with two hooks to the left.	Stem, with three hooks to the left.

What is the use of a Dot after any Note, or Rest?

A Dot is equal to half the preceding Note: consequently, a Whole Note with a Dot is equal to three Half Notes. A half Note with a Dot is equal to three Quarter Notes.

A Quarter Note with a Dot is as long as three Eighth Notes; thus:

What is a Triplet?

When *three* Eighth Notes, instead of *two*, are played to a Quarter Note, or *three* Sixteenths, instead of *two*, to an Eighth, they are called Triplets; and in the same proportion to all other Notes. Triplets are generally, but not always, marked with a figure of 3. The figure 3 is usually placed over the first group of Notes only.

What is a Double Triplet?

It is called a Double Triplet, when *six* Eighth Notes are played in the time of *four*, or in the time of a Half Note; or when *six* Sixteenth Notes are played in the time of *four*, &c. The figure of 6 is usually placed over the first group of Notes.

CHAPTER III.

OF TIME.

What are Bars ?

Short Lines drawn across the Staff, to divide the Music into equal portions ; but the Music between two of these is also called a Bar or Measure.

How many sorts of Time are there?

Two : Common Time, and Triple Time.

What is meant by Common Time?

An even number of parts in a Bar, as Two, Four, Six, or Twelve.

What is meant by Triple Time?

An odd number of parts, as Three or Nine.

How is the Time marked?

At the beginning of every piece of Music ; sometimes it is marked by a C which signifies Common Time, and the Bar then contains the value of a Semibreve, but generally expressed four Crochets in a Bar : the Time is also occasionally marked by two Figures, which have a reference to the Semibreve.

How do the Figures refer to the Semibreve?

The lowest Figure shows into how many parts the Semibreve is divided, and the upper Figure shows how many of those parts are to be in a Bar.

Name the Divisions of a Semibreve.

A Semibreve divided into two parts, will become Minims: divided into four parts, it will become Crochets: divided into eight parts, it will become Quavers: consequently, the figure of 2, represents Minims ; the figure of 4, represents Crochets ; and the figure of 8 represents Quavers.

Explain the following marks of Time: pointing out which are Common and which are Triple Time.

C | $\frac{2}{4}$ | $\frac{6}{8}$ | $\frac{12}{4}$ | $\frac{12}{8}$ | $\frac{3}{2}$

$\frac{9}{8}$ | $\frac{3}{4}$ | $\frac{6}{4}$ | $\frac{9}{4}$ | $\frac{3}{8}$

How many sorts of Common and Triple Times are there?

Two of each, viz; Simple and Compound.

How are they distinguished?

The easiest way is to remember, that if the Number of Notes expressed by the upper figure, or figures, is less than 6, it is Simple; but if it is 6, or more than 6, it is Compound.

Explain again all the marks of Time, pointing out which are Simple and which are Compound.

Is it necessary to count the Time exactly as expressed by the Figures?

No. Two Crotchets may be counted as four Quavers; three Crotchets as six Quavers, &c.

How is the Time to be counted, if the piece contains Triplets?

It must be counted by the value of the Triplet: for example, if there are three Quavers to a Crotchet, the Time must be counted by Crotchets: if there are three Semiquavers to a Quaver, it must be counted by Quavers.

OF MEASURE, TIME, ETC., NEWLY EXPLAINED.

What are Bars?

Short Lines drawn across the Staff, to divide the Music into Measures.

What is a Measure?

The quantity of Music contained between two Bars.

How many kinds of Measure are there?

There are four principal kinds of Measure in general use, viz: *Two-fold*, or *Double*; *Three-fold*, or *Triple*; *Four-fold*, or *Quadruple*; and the *Six-fold*, or *Sextuple*.

What is meant by Two-fold, or Double Measure?

An even number of parts in a Measure, as *two halves*, or *two quarters*. It is accented on the first part of the Measure.

What is meant by Three-fold, or Triple Measure?

An *odd* number of parts in a Measure, as *three halves*, or *three quarters*, or *three eighths*. It is accented on the first part of the Measure.

What is meant by Four-fold, or Quadruple Measure?

An *even* number of parts in a Measure, as *four halves*, *four quarters*, or *four eighths*. It is accented on the first and third parts of the Measure.

What is meant by Six-fold, or Sextuple Measure?

An *even* number of parts in a Measure, each part containing an *odd* number, as *six quarters* divided into twice three, or *six eighths* divided into twice three. It is accented on the first and fourth parts of the Measure,

Are there any other Measures used?

Yes: the Nine-fold and Twelve-fold are sometimes used.

What is meant by Nine-fold Measure?

An *odd* number of parts in a Measure, each part containing an *odd* number, as *nine quarters*, or *nine eighths* divided into three times three. It is accented on the first, fourth and seventh parts of the Measure.

What is meant by Twelve-fold Measure?

An *odd* number of parts in a Measure, each part containing an *even* number, as *twelve quarters*, or *twelve eighths*, divided into three times four. It is accented on the first, fifth, and ninth parts of the Measure.

How is Time marked?

The Time is marked at the beginning of every piece of Music, either by two figures, or by the letter C

How is Two-fold, or Double Time expressed?

By the figures $\frac{2}{2}$, $\frac{2}{4}$, and sometimes $\frac{2}{1}$ or $\frac{2}{8}$.

How is Three-fold, or Triple Time expressed?

By the figures $\frac{3}{2}$, $\frac{3}{4}$ or $\frac{3}{8}$.

How is Four-fold, or Quadruple Time expressed?

By the figures $\frac{4}{2}$, $\frac{4}{4}$; or by the sign 𝄵, which signifies Common Time.

How is Six fold, or Sextuple Time expressed?

By the figures $\frac{6}{8}$ or $\frac{6}{4}$.

How are Nine-fold and Twelve-fold Time expressed?

Nine-fold Time is expressed by the figures $\frac{9}{8}$ or $\frac{9}{4}$; and Twelve-fold Time, by the figures $\frac{12}{8}$ or $\frac{12}{4}$.

How do the figures refer to the Whole Note?

The *lower* figure shows into how many parts the Whole Note is divided, and the *upper* figure, or figures, show how many of those parts are to be in a measure

---

CHAPTER IV.

OF THE POSITION OF THE HAND, AND MANNER OF PLAYING, ETC.

In what position should the hand and arm be held?

The hand and arm should be even, neither raising nor depressing the wrist: the fingers should be bent at the middle joint, so as to bring the points of them even with the end of the thumb.

How many Keys should be covered by the hand in its natural position?

Five; one finger over the centre of each Key. In pressing down a Key with one finger, care must be taken not to move the others.

How many Keys are to be held down at one time?

Generally speaking, one, and that must be kept down

until the next Key is struck, but not longer. When two or more Keys are struck at one time, they are considered but as one, and they must be held down until the next Keys are struck.

In what cases should the fingers be raised?

When any Key is struck more than once, it should be raised every time but the last; and the fingers must of course be raised whenever a Rest appears.

What is the meaning of playing *Legato*?

It signifies playing smoothly, always keeping one Key down until the next be struck.

What is playing *Staccato*?

Separating the Notes from each other, or raising the finger from one Key before the other is down.

What is a Slur? ⁀ ‿

It is a curved line, drawn over, or under two or more Notes to signify that they are to be played Legato.

What is a Tie, or Bind? ‿ ⁀

It is of the same form as a Slur, but placed to two Notes alike: it binds the second to the first, so that only the first is to be struck; but the finger must be held down the full time of both,

How are Notes marked which are to be played Staccato?

With round dots or pointed specks, above or below them: those with dots are to be played moderately staccato; those with specks, very much so.

Play the following passage, in the three different ways it is marked.

How are Notes to be played which are marked with Dots and Slurs also?

On a repetition of the same Note, they should be played as closely as possible.

When Notes, thus marked, are played in succession, the fingers should be gently put down and gently raised.

CHAPTER V.

OF SHARPS, FLATS, ETC.

What is an Interval?

An Interval is the difference or distance between two sounds.

What is the smallest Interval?

A Semitone, or half a Tone. Each Key of the Piano-Forte is a Semitone from that which is next to it, whether it be a White Key or a black one.

What is a Sharp? ♯

A Sharp placed before any Note, raises it one Semitone, or to the next Key on the right hand.

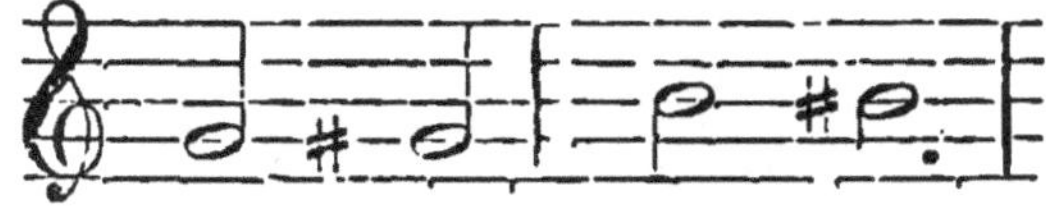

What is a Flat? ♭

A Flat placed before any Note, lowers it one Semitone or to the next Key on the left hand

What is a natural? ♮

A Natural brings a Note that has been raised by a Sharp, or lowered by a Flat, to its former place again.

consequently, a Natural sometimes raises and sometimes lowers a Note.

Why are Sharps or Flats placed at the beginning of a piece of music?

Any Sharps or Flats placed at the beginning affect all notes of the corresponding names, throughout the piece.

For example, a Sharp on ♯ the fifth line signifies that all the F's are to be played Sharp; and Flats upon the third Line and fourth ♭ ♭ Space, signify that all the B's and E's are to be Flat.

What are Accidental Sharps, Flats or Naturals?

Accidentals are those which are not marked at the beginning of the piece.

How long does the influence of an Accidental last?

An Accidental affects all Notes of the same name in the Bar. For Example,

signifies that all the C's are to be sharp, though only the first is marked.

The Flat in this Example, although placed to B on the third Line, affects the B above the first Ledger Line.

Do Accidentals ever affect Notes in the Bar following?

Yes; if the last Note of one Bar, which has been made sharp, begins the next, it is to continue sharp.

The same is to be observed of Flats and Naturals.

CHAPTER VI.

OF COMMON CHARACTERS USED IN MUSIC.

What is the use of Double Bars?

Double Bars are placed in the middle, or at the end of a piece of Music, to show that a part, or the whole is finished.

What is the use of Dots at a Bar, or at a Double Bar?

They signify, that that part of the Music which is on the same side as the Dots, is to be repeated. For Example, these Dots being on  the left-hand side of the Double Bar, signify that the Performer, is to repeat the former piece: but  these Dots being on the right-hand side, signify that the Performer, after having played to the next Dot. is to return to this place.

What is the use of a Sign? $.

The second time it occurs in a piece of Music, it is generally accompanied with the words '*Dal Segno,*' which signify '*From the Sign;*' consequently, the Performer, is to return to the first mark.

What is the meaning of *Da Capo?*—generally abbreviated *D. C.*

From the beginning.

What is the meaning of *Da Capo al Segno?*

From the beginning at the Sign.

Why are the Fgures 1 and 2, sometimes placed at the Double Bar, in the middle of a Movement?

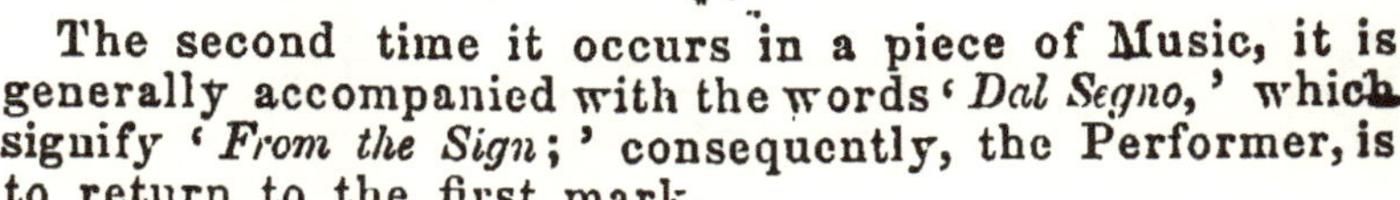

The Dots at the Double Bar show that the piece is to be repeated; and the Figures denote that the Performer, in playing it through the second time, is to omit the Bar marked 1, and play that which is marked 2 instead.

What is the use of a Pause?

A Pause placed over a Note, signifies that the finger is to be held down, and the Performer is to pause as long as he thinks proper.

A Pause over a Rest has the same meaning, excepting that the fingers are to be raised.

Why is a Pause sometimes placed over a Double Bar?

A Pause, (or the words *Il Fine*,) placed at a Double Bar, shows that the piece is to end at that place, after the *Da Capo*.

What is the meaning of the word *Bis?*

It is generally accompanied with Dots at the Bars, and placed under a Slur; it signifies, that the passage over which it is placed, is to be played twice over.

What is the use of a Direct?

It is placed at the end of a Staff, or at the bottom of a page, to indicate the name of the following Note.

What is the meaning of *Volti Subito?* generally marked *V. S.*

Volti, means turn over; *Subito*, quickly.

What is the meaning of *Ottava Alta?* generally marked 8va.----

It signifies, that the Music over which it is placed, is to be played an Octave higher, as far as the marks of continuation extend.

What is the meaning of *Loco?*

It signifies, that the Music is to be played as it is written; that is to say, no longer an Octave higher.

The Pupil should now be exercised in naming the Keys of the Piano-Forte, without looking at the Instrument, remarking that the Black Keys are occasionally called Sharps, and occasionally Flats. (See Appendix, Exercise I.) The White Keys, also, commonly called E F, and B, C, frequently change their names, and are used as Flats or Sharps to their neighboring Keys. The others too, are occasionally called Double Sharps and Double Flats, which are explained at the beginning of Chapter XI. (See also, Appendix, Exercise II.)

Name a Chromatic Semitone* above A, A, ♯, &c. &c.

A Chromatic Semitone above A is A♯; a Chromatic Semitone above A♯ is A𝄪, &c., &c.

Name a Diatonic Semitone above A, B, &c. (See Appendix, Exercise XIII, page 53.)

Name a Diatonic Semitone below A, B, &c. (See Appendix, Exercise XIII, page 53.)

CHAPTER VII.

OF GRACES, AND COMMON MARKS OF EXPRESSION.

What is an Appogiatura?

It is a small Note prefixed to a large one, from which it generally takes half its time. For example, an Appogiatura

before a Minim, must be played as a Crochet,

consequently it does not lengthen the Bar.

When an Appogiatura is placed before a Double Note, is it to be played by itself, (as it appears,) or with the lower Note?

The Appogiatura is to be played instead of part of the upper Note; consequently, the lower Note must be played with it. For example,

* For an explanation of the difference between a Chromatic and a Diatonic Semitone, see page 43.

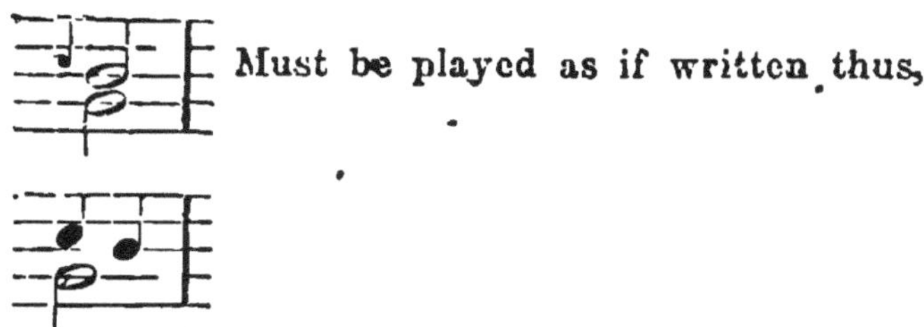

Are all Appogiaturas to be made half the time of the Note they precede?

No: they, as well as the other Graces used in Music, depend greatly on the taste and judgment of the performer; consequently, they can be best explained as they occur.

How is a Turn ~ to be made?

A Turn is to be made with the Note above, and the Note below that which is written, beginning with the highest; consequently, a Turn upon C, will be made with D, C, B, C.

Should the lowest Note of a Turn be a Tone, or a Semitone below the Note written?

In most cases it should be a Semitone.

Supposing a Turn be made upon A; is it immaterial whether it be called B, A, G♯ A, or B, A, A♭, A?

No: three different letters must be made use of in a Turn; therefore the lowest must be called G♯, and not A♭,

Name, write or play a Turn upon A, upon B. C, D, E, F, G, &c.

How is a Turn made upon a Dotted Note?

By first striking the Note itself, and making the Turn afterwards,

What is an inverted Turn?

An inverted Turn consists of the *same* Notes as a Turn; but beginning with the lowest instead of the highest Note.

Make an inverted Turn upon A, B, C, D, E, F, G, &c.

How is a Shake to be made?

A Shake is made with the Note above, and the Note which is written; beginning with the highest, and concluding with a Turn. For Example:

Must be played

Or thus,

The rapidity of the Shake depending on the ability of the Performer.

Make a Shake upon A, B, C, D, E. F, G, &c.

What is the meaning of Piano?

Soft; generally abreviated *Pia,* or *P.*

What is Pianissimo?

Very soft; generally abbreviated *PPmo,* or *PP.*

What is the meaning of Forte?

Loud; generally abbreviated *For.* or *F.*

What is Fortissimo?

Very loud; generally marked *ffmo.* or *ff.*

What is the meaning of Mezzo Forte, and Mezzo Piano?

Mezzo Forte signifies moderately loud, and Mezzo Piano moderately soft; they are generally marked *Mf.* and *mp.*

What is the meaning of Dolce, or Dol.?

Softly, or sweetly.

What is the meaning of Tenuto, or Teno.?

It signifies that the fingers are to be particularly held down during the passage to which it is applied.

What is Forzando, or Sforzato?

They each signify that one Note is to be played strong; they are abbreviated *fz.* and *sf.*

What is Rinforzando?

It signifies that several Notes are to be played strong: it is generally marked *rinf.* or *rf.*

What is the meaning of Crescendo, or Cres.?

Begin softly, and gradually increase the sound. The following mark

is also occasionally used to signify that the Performer is to play Piano where it is small, and Forte where it is large. If a small mark of this sort > is applied to one Note, it has the same effect as fz.

What is the meaning of Diminuendo, or Decrescendo?

Begin loud, and gradually diminish the sound. They are generally marked dim. or decres. or

What is the meaning of Calando, or Cal.?

Gradually softer and slower.

What is the meaning of Perdendosi?

It has the same meaning as Calando.

What is the meaning of a Tempo, or Tempo Primo?

After having slackened the Time at Calando, it signifies that the original Time is to be resumed.

What is the meaning of ad libitum, or ad lib.?

It signifies 'at pleasure;' that is to say the Performer may play the passage as it is written, or introduce any Cadence he thinks proper.

When two Notes are marked with a Slur, thus,

In what manner are they to be played?

As if marked thus, that is to say, the first is to be pressed and held down, the second played softly, and the finger raised immediately.

What is meant by a curved or waved Line placed before a Chord?

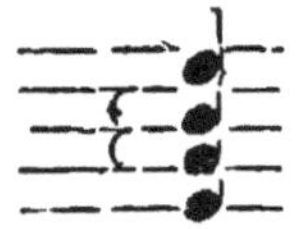

It signifies that the Notes are not to be played quite together, but successively from the lowest upwards. Chords played in this manner are called spread.

CHAPTER VII.

OF INTERVALS.

What is an Interval?

An Interval is the difference or distance between two sounds. It must be remembered, that all Intervals are called according to the degrees of the Staff, or according to the number of letters they are distant from each other.

For instance is a *Second*;

a Sharp *Second*: but if the same Keys

are struck, and called the interval is then

called a *Third*.

Are Intervals to be reckoned upwards or downwards?

Always upwards from the Note named, unless the contrary be expressed,

What is a Tone?

It consists of two Semitones. The Interval between F and F♯, is one Semitone; and between F♯ and G, is another. For Example,

consequently, the Interval between F and G is a whole Tone.*

What is a Minor, or lesser Third?

A Minor Third (sometimes improperly called a Flat Third) is three Semitones from the Note named. For example, the Minor Third of A, must be reckoned thus: from A to A ♯ *one* Semitone, to B *two*, to C *three*.

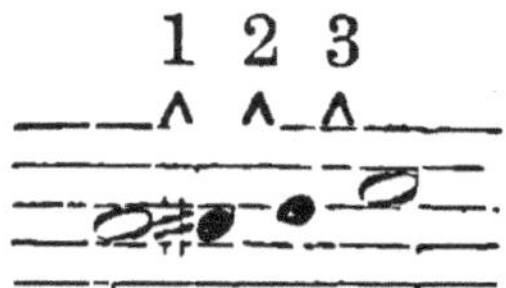

How many Semitones is a Major, or Greater Third from the Note named?

Four: (this Interval is sometimes improperly called a Sharp Third.)

As the Semitone above C, may be called either C♯ or D♭, is it immaterial in reckoning the Major Third of A, whether you say C♯ or D♭?

No: the Major *Third* of A, must be called C♯. For example, A, B, C, is a *Third*, and A, B, C, D, is a Fourth.

Name, write, or play Minor and Major Thirds† to A, B, C, D, E, F, G;

*The Pupil should be required to *prove* all Intervals, by inserting (or counting) the Semitones in this manner.

†In reckoning Thirds, or any other Intervals, the Pupil is recommended first to fix upon the proper letter, and afterwards ascertain (by counting the Semitones) whether the letter fixed upon, is to be Natural, Sharp, Double Sharp, Flat, or Double Flat. For example, after having decided that the Third of A must be C, it remains to be proved which of the five C's (viz: C♮, C♯, C𝄪, C♭, C♭♭) is the one required. That C, which is three Semitones from A is the Minor Third, and that C, which is four Semitones from A, is the Major Third.

to A#, B#, C#, D#, E#, &c.; to Ab, Bb, Cb, Db, Eb, &c.

How many Semitones is a perfect fifth from the Note named?

Seven:

but the easiest way is to remember, that every Note, excepting one, has a Fifth either Sharp, Flat, or Natural, like itself. For example, the Fifth of C is G, the Fifth of C *sharp*, is G *sharp*, the Fifth of C *flat* is G *flat*.

What Note has a Fifth unlike itself?

B; the Fifth of which must be raised a Semitone to make it perfect. For example, the Fifth of B is F *sharp*, the Fifth of B *sharp* is F✕, the Fifth of B *flat* is F.

Name or write Fifths to all the Notes, beginning with F, and proceeding always a Fifth higher.

F, C, G, D, A, E, B, F *sharp*, C *sharp*, G *sharp*, D *sharp*, A *sharp*, E *sharp*, B *sharp*, F ✕, C ✕, &c.

Name Fifths to Flats now, commencing with F *Flat*.

F *flat*, C *flat*, G *flat*, D *flat*, A *flat*, E *flat*, B *flat*, F♮, &c.

By way of exercise, now name the Fifths below, and observe that in reckoning downwards, every Note has a Fifth like itself, excepting F, the Fifth below which must be lowered a Semitone. For example, the Fifth below F is B *flat*, the Fifth below F *flat* is B *double flat*, the Fifth below F# is B

B, E, A, E, G, C, F, B *flat*, E *flat*, A *flat*, D *flat*, G *flat*. C *flat*, F *flat*, B *double flat*, &c.

Name the Fifths below to the Sharps, commencing with B *sharp*.

B *sharp*, E *sharp*, A *sharp*, D *sharp*, G *sharp*, C *sharp*, F *sharp*, B *natural*. &c.

Name again the two Letters which have Fifths, not Sharp, Flat or Natural, like themselves

B, in reckoning Fifths upwards; and F, in reckoning Fifths downwards.

What is the *Leading Note*?

The Leading Note is the Sharp *Seventh* of the Scale: it is eleven Semitones from the Note named; but the easiest way is to reckon it one Semitone below the Octave.

As you say *Sharp Seventh*, is the leading *Note* always a Sharp?

No. For example, the Leading Note of F, is E *natural*; the Leading Note of A, is G *sharp*; and the Leading Note of C *flat*, is B *flat*.*

As the Leading Note is one Semitone below the Octave, is it immaterial whether the Leading Note of A be called G *sharp* or A *flat*?

No: for although A *flat* is a Semitone below the Octave, it is the *eighth* letter or Degree, and the Leading Note must be the *seventh*.

Name or write the Leading Note of A; of B, C, D, E, F, G? of A *sharp*, B *sharp*, C *sharp*, D *sharp*, E *sharp*, F *sharp* G *sharp*; A *flat*, B *flat*, C *flat*, D *flat*, E *flat*, F *flat*. G *flat*.

Name or write Minor Thirds, Major Thirds, Fifths and Leading Notes to A, B, C. D, E, F, G; A *sharp*, B *sharp* C, *sharp*, D *sharp*, E *sharp*, F *sharp*, G *sharp*; A *flat*, B *flat*, C *flat*, D *flat*, E *flat*, F *flat*, G *flat*.

Name or write Minor Thirds, Major Thirds, Fifths, and Leading Notes to A *flat*, B *sharp*, C, D *flat*, E *sharp*, F, G *flat*, ; A *sharp*, B, C *flat*, D *sharp*, E, F *flat*, G *sharp*; A, B *flat*, C *sharp*, D, E *flat*, F *sharp*, G.

* In naming Intervals in general, it is sufficient to name the letter, if a Natural be intended. Thus it is sufficient to say that the Minor Third of A is C, and not to say C *natural*: but in naming or writing Leading Notes, it should be always expressed; the Leading Note of B *flat* is A *natural*, the Leading Note of E *flat* is D *natural*, &c. This is recommended that the Pupil may hereafter more readily find the Leading Notes of the Minor Keys, which are already marked with an Accidental Sharp, Flat, or Natural

CHAPTER IX.

OF THE SIGNATURE.

How do you determine what is the *Tonic*, or *Key Note* of a piece of Music?

Principally by the Signature, or number of Sharps or Flats at the beginning.

What method have you of discovering the Tonic?

Every Tonic, or Key Note, is a fifth higher for every additional Flat, commencing always with C, which Key has neither Flat nor Sharp.

Name the order of Keys with Sharps.

C has no Sharp, G has one, D has two, A has three, E has four, B has five, F♯ has six, and C♯ has seven.

Name the order of Keys with Flats.

C has no Flat. F has one, B♭ has two, E♭ has three, A♭ has four, D♭ has five, G♭ has six, and C♭ has seven.

What Key has two (or more) Sharps (or Flats,) &c.

What is the Signature, (or number of Sharps or Flats) of the Key A, D *flat*, F *sharp*, &c. &c.

How many Keys have the same Signature?

There are *two* of each. For example, every Tonic, or Key Note, has its relative Minor.*

How is the Relative Minor of any Key to be found?

The Relative Minor of every Key is a Minor Third below. For example, the Relative Minor of C, is A Minor; the Relative Minor of B♭, is G Minor.

Name the Relative Minor of C, of G, D A, E, B, F *sharp*, C *sharp*; of C, F, B *flat*, E *flat*, A *flat*, D *flat*, G *flat*, and C *flat*.

In what manner do you decide whether a piece is in the Key which is indicated by the Signature, or in its Relative Minor?

By looking for the Leading Note of the Minor Key alluded to; as the Leading Note of every Minor Key is marked with an Accidental Sharp or Natural. For example,

* The difference between Major and Minor Keys will be more fully explained hereafter: the present is only given as the *readiest* way of enabling a Pupil to ascertain what Key any piece of Music is in.

Judging from the Signature, this may be either in C, or A Minor, but as the first G is Sharp, (which is the Leading Note of A,) the piece is in the Key of A Minor.

This piece, having one Sharp at the Signature may be either in G, or E Minor; but as the first D is not Sharp, it cannot be in E Minor; consequently, it is in the Key of G.

Is this an invariable Rule for ascertaining what Key a piece of Music is in?

No; exceptions to it (though very seldom) may be met with; but these can only be understood by those who study harmony.

Name or write the order of Keys with Sharps and Flats; also the Relative Minor, and the Leading Note of the Relative Minor, to each Key.

As the Relative Minor of any Key is a Minor Third below, of course, the Relative Major of any Minor Key is a Minor Third above; name, therefore, the Relative Major of A Minor, &c. &c.

CHAPTER X.

OF THE FORMATION OF THE SCALE.

What is a Tetrachord?

A Tetrachord is composed of four Sounds, placed at the Intervals of two Tones and one Semitone; that is to say, the Interval between the first and second Sound must be a Tone; between the second and third, a Tone; and between the third and fourth, a Semitone.

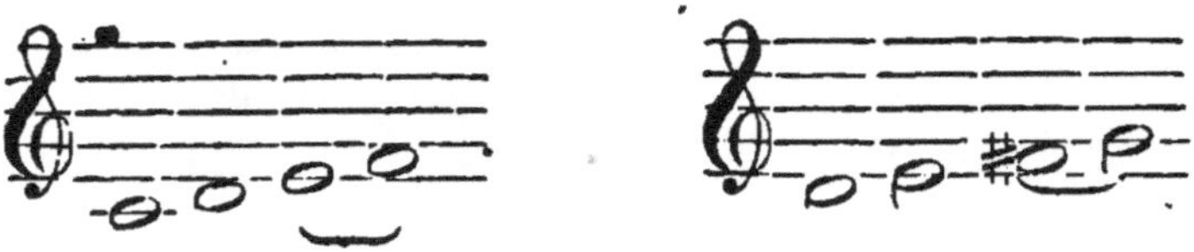

Make Tetrachords, commencing with F ; A *sharp* ; B *flat* ; F *flat*. Mark the Semitones with a Slur.

Make descending Tetrachords, commencing with A ; B *flat* ; F *flat* ; B *double flat* ; and observe that the interval of the Semitone must still be between the two highest Sounds of the Tetrachord.

What is the Diatonic Scale ?

The Diatonic Scale must consist of the seven Letters or Degrees, and the Octave to the first, in regular succession, proceeding by Tones and Semitones.

How do you form the Diatonic Scale ?

By making two Tetrachords, leaving the Interval of one Tone between them, called the Tone of Disjunction.

Form the Scale of C Mark the Semitones with a Slur, and Separate the Tetrachords, at the tone of Disjunction, by a Bar.

Lower Tetrachord. Upper Tetrachord.

It is to be remarked, that the Semitones are between the Third and Fourth, and between the Seventh and Eighth of the Scale. In all Major Keys, the ascending and descending Scales are composed of the same Notes.

Name every interval of the foregoing Scale.

C, is the Tonic, or Key Note ; D, the second ; E, the third ; F, the fourth, &c. &c.*

Make the Scale of E *sharp*, the Scale of G *flat*.

Make the descending Scale of A, *flat*, F, *sharp*.

In what manner are Scales to be formed, so as to shew their connexion with each other, and to shew the order of the Seven Sharps ?

*The Pupil should be required to name the Intervals of every Scale that is formed.

Commence with the Scale of C, and take the upper Tetrachord of one Scale for the lower Tetrachord of the next. Observe, that every Scale will be a Fifth higher than the preceding and will have an additional Sharp.

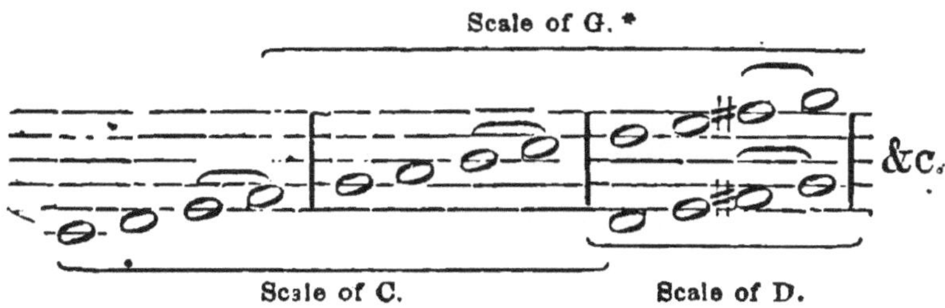

Make Scales* progressively; mark the first and each succeeding Sharp upon a separate Staff, until you have found the order of the seven Sharps. viz:

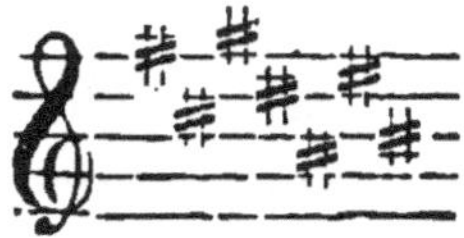

After having found the order of Sharps regularly, by making Scales, the Pupil will do well to remember, that F is the first, and that every succeeding Sharp is a Fifth higher.

In what manner are Scales to be formed, so as to shew the order of the Flats?

Exactly the reverse of the former; that is to say, the lower Tetrachord of one Scale must be taken for the upper Tetrachord of the next. For example, the lower Tetrachord of C, is the upper one of F.

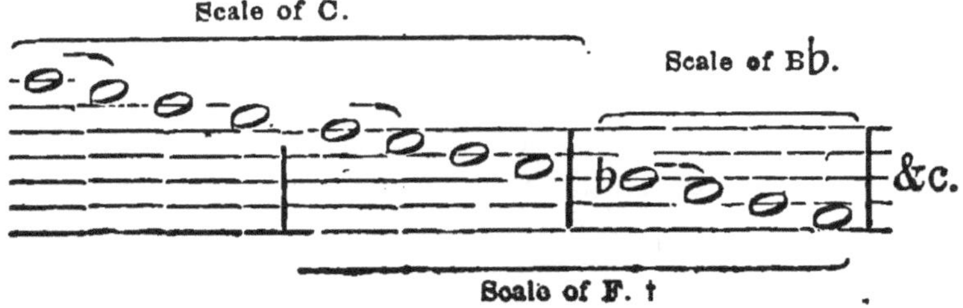

*In order to avoid the inconvenience of the Ledger Lines, it will be necessary, in commencing the succeeding Scales, to copy the Notes of the alternate Tetrachords an Octave lower.

†In order to avoid the inconvenience of the Ledger Lines, it will be ne

Make Scales progressively; mark the first and each succeeding Flat upon a separate Staff, until you have found the order of the seven Flats, viz :

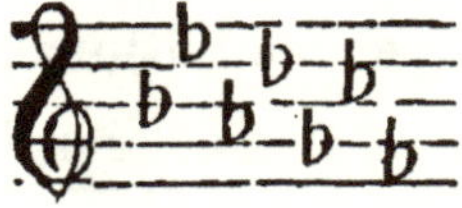

After having found the order of Flats regularly, by forming the Scales the Pupil will do well to remember, that B is the first Flat, and that every succeeding Flat is a Fifth lower.

What is meant by the Dominant and Subdominant?

The Dominant signifies the fifth above. and the Subdominant the Fifth below. Every Scale is intimately connected with the Scales of its Dominant and Subdominant.

Form the Scale of ——— with its Dominant and Subdominant.

What is the difference between a Major Key and a Minor Key?

A Major Key signifies, that the *Third* of the Scale is a Major Third from the Tonic; and a Minor Key signifies, that the *Third* is a Minor Third from the Tonic.

Key of C Major, or Key of C, with a Major Third.

Key of A Minor, or Key of A, with a Minor Third.

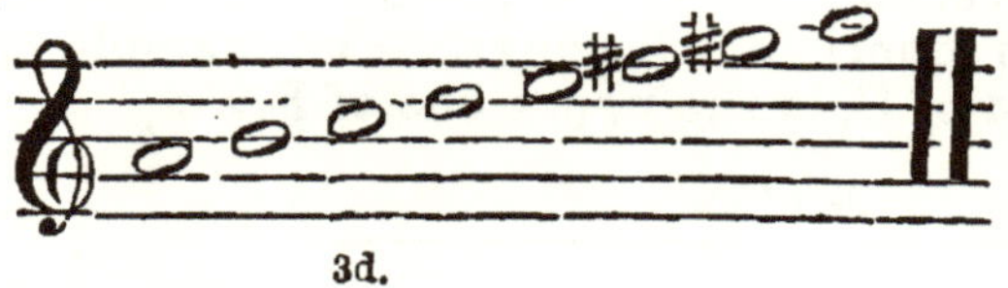

What is the Minor Scale.

The Minor Scale consists of the same number of Tones and Semitones of the Major, (viz: five whole Tones and two Semitones,) but differently disposed; the *ascending* also, differs from the *descending* Scale. For example, A is the Relative Minor of C, and has neither Flat nor Sharp at the Signature.

cessary, in commencing the succeeding Scales, to copy the Notes of the alternate Tetrachords an Octave higher.

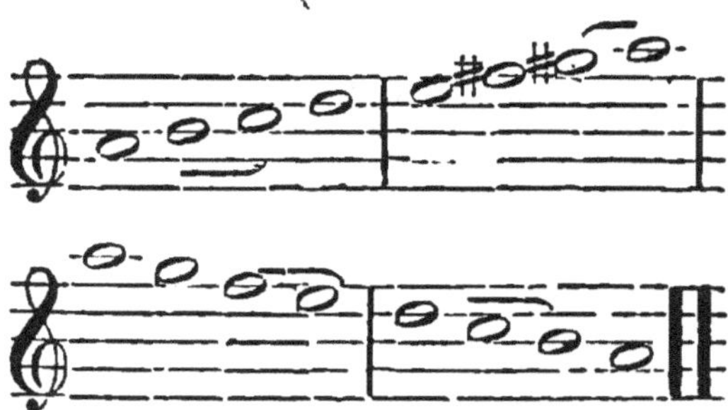

The Semitones, it is to be observed, are not in the same situations as in the Major Scale.

How is the Minor Scale to be formed?

The easiest way is to form it with the *same* Flats or Sharps as its Relative Major, remembering, that the Sixth and Seventh of the Ascending Scale must each be raised a Semitone by Accidental Sharps or Naturals. For example, D is the Relative Minor of F; consequently, must have B *flat* at the Signature. The Sixth and Seventh, as has been before remarked, are raised by Accidentals, in the Ascending Scale.

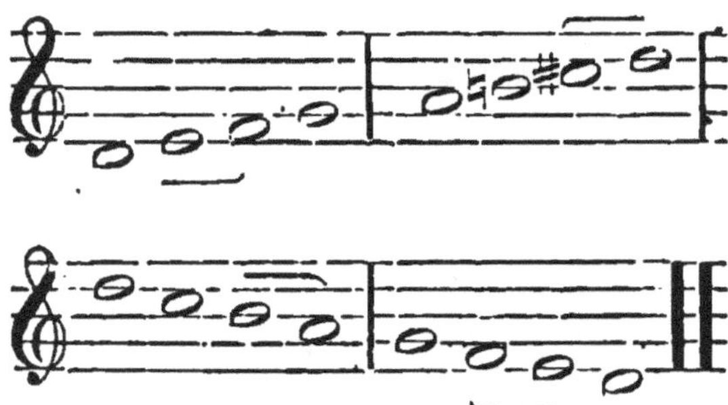

Why are the Sixth and Seventh Notes of the Ascending Minor Scale raised by Accidentals?

The Seventh is raised, because every Ascending Scale must have a Leading Note; and the Sixth is also raised, that the Interval between the Sixth and Seventh may not be greater than a Tone; for the Diatonic Scale must consist of Tones and Semitones.

Repeat the Method of making a Minor Scale.

First ascertain what is its Relative Major; secondly, write the Signature; thirdly, write the Scale ascending and descending; fourthly, raise the Sixth and Seventh of the ascending Scale, each one Semitone.

Write the Scale of D Minor, G Minor. F *sharp* Minor, B Minor, C Minor, &c,

Write the Scale of the Relative Minor of D, E, D *flat*, C *sharp*, &c.

Write the Scales of the *Relative Minors* to C, G, D, A, E, B, F *sharp*, C *sharp*, C, F, B *flat*, F *flat*, A *flat*, D *flat*, C *flat*.

What is the Chromatic Scale?

The Chromatic Scale consists of Semitones only.

Is it immaterial, in writing the Chromatic Scale, whether you write A *flat*, or G *sharp*, and A *sharp*, or B *flat*?

No; the Signatures must be attended to. For example, with three Flats, you must not write

but every Note should have its proper situation on the Staff, according to the Signature: thus,

This renders fewer Accidentals necessary.

By way of Exercise, write the same passage as above with four Sharps at the Signature.

In order to draw the attention to the subject of fingering, it is now recommended that the Pupil should write and finger all the Scales, commencing with the Scale of C, and going on progressively as far as the Scale of C *sharp*, and the Scale of C *flat*, ascending and descending two octaves both for the right hand and the left. These should be first written upon a slate fingered, and when corrected by the master, copied into a book for daily practice. The Major Scales should be written on one side of the book, and their relative Minors on the opposite page. The proper Sharps or Flats belonging to each Scale should be placed as the signature at the beginning, and not as they occur in the Scale, excepting of course the sixth and seventh of the Minor Scales, which require raising by accidentals in the ascending, and contradicting (on account of being written without Bars) in the descending Scale.

In fingering the Scales, the following remarks may be found useful.

The fingering is only to be marked upon the first note of the Scale, and where the thumb is to be passed under the fingers, or the fingers over the thumb.

In the ascending Scale of two octaves for the right hand—commence with the thumb—pass the thumb under the second finger—next under the third finger, and again under the second, which will prepare sufficient fingers to ascend to the top of the Scale.

In descending, commence with the fourth finger—pass the second finger over the thumb—next pass the third finger over, and lastly the second finger over.

When the Scale commences with a Black Key commence with the first finger, and follow the foregoing rule as closely as the situation of the Black Keys will admit of; observing that neither the thumb nor the fourth finger must be placed upon a Black Key in fingering a Scale.

In the ascending Scale of two octaves for the left hand commence with the fourth finger—pass the second finger over the thumb—next pass the third finger, and lastly the second finger.

In descending commence with the thumb—pass the thumb under the second finger, next under the third finger, and lastly under the second finger.

The situation of the Black Keys will render it necessary to commence in some Scales with the third, second, or first finger, instead of the fourth but the foregoing rule is to be followed as closely as circumstances will admit of.

No Scale should be practised till it has been inspected by the Master.

Nothing can be more generally useful than the daily practice of the Scales, at the same time the greatest attention is requisite on the part of the Pupil to the position and steadiness of the hand, as well as to the clearness and connexion of the Notes. (See Chap. IV.)

CHAPTER XI.

OF VARIOUS CHARACTERS USED IN MUSIC,

What is a Double Sharp? ✕

A Double Sharp raises a Note two Semitones.

What is a Double Flat? ♭♭

A Double Flat lowers a Note two Semitones.

How is a Single Sharp or Flat replaced after a Double one?

By means of a Natural and Sharp, or a Natural and Flat.

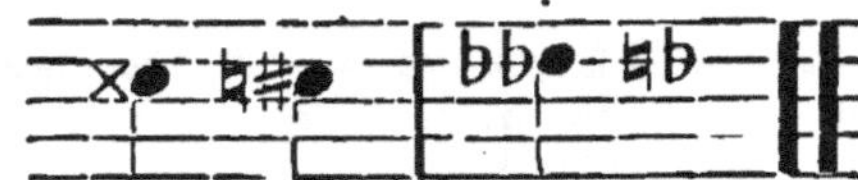

As a Dot after a Note makes it half as long again, what is the use of a second Dot?

The second Dot is equal to half the first; consequently, a Crotchet with two Dots, is equal to a Crotchet, Quaver, and Semiquaver.

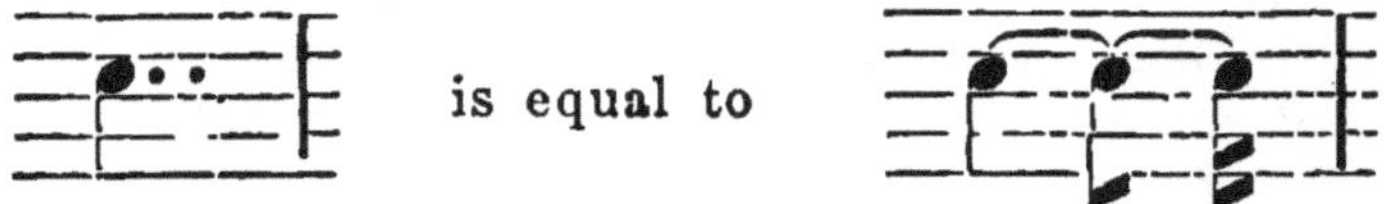

As *Semi* signifies half, and *Breve* short, why is the longest Note calle a Semibreve?

A Semibreve is the longest in *present* use: but there were two others formerly called a

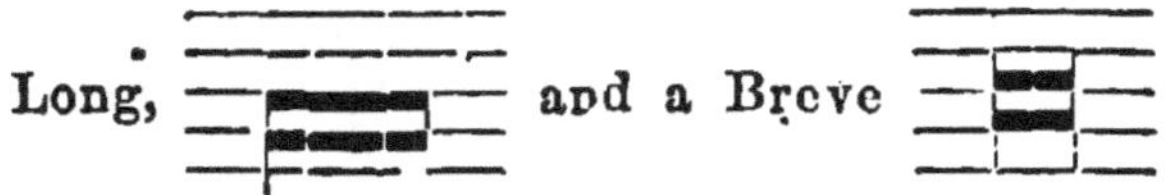

What proportion dces a Semibreve bear to them?

A Long is equal to two Breves, or four Semibreves; consequently, a Semibreve is equal to half a Breve, or a quarter of a Long.

Is a Demisemiquaver the shortest Note?

No: there is one called a half Demisemiquaver, made thus, and its Rest thus, sixty-four of these are equal to one Semibreve.

In what manner is a whole Bar Rest marked?

In the same manner as a Semibreve Rest, be the value of the Bar what it may.

In what manner are Rests for more than one Bar marked?

A Rest for two Bars is made from one line to the next; for four Bars, from one line to the next but one; but a Figure expressive of the number of Bars, is frequently placed over; and when the number is very great, Figures only are used.

In what manner do you count several Bars' Rest?

By naming the number, instead of the word One on the first of each Bar. For example,

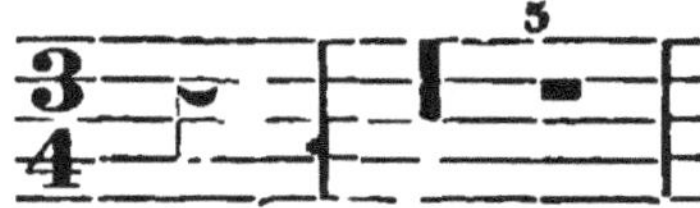

These five Bars' Rests should be counted.

1, 2, 3, | 2, 2, 3, | 3, 2, 3, | 4, 2, 3, |
instead of always one, two, three.

What is melody?

A Melody is a succession of Sounds.

What is Harmony?

A combination of Sounds.

Are there any more Clefs than the Treble and the Base?

Yes: the C Clef, This Clef is occasionally placed upon either of the four lowest lines of the Staff, and gives the name of C to all Notes on the same line as itself; the other Notes are, of course, named by degrees from it; its situation on the Piano-Forte is the middle C.

When this Clef is placed upon the first line, it is called

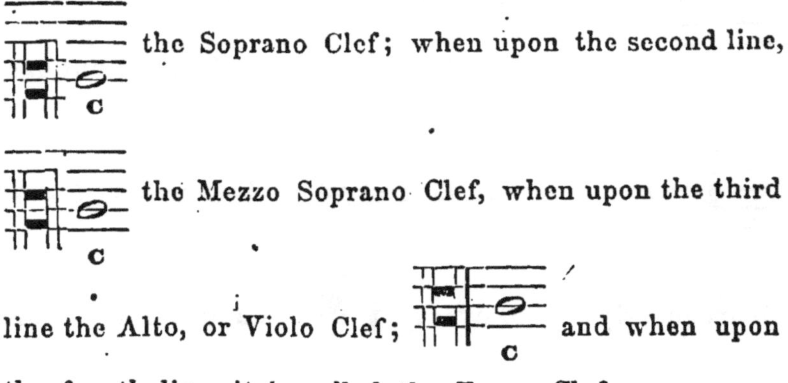

the Soprano Clef; when upon the second line, the Mezzo Soprano Clef, when upon the third line the Alto, or Violo Clef; and when upon the fourth line, it is called the Tenor Clef.

Name all the Degrees of the Staff, according to these Clefs.

Do the Treble and Base Clefs ever change their situations on the Staff?

Yes, in very old Music: but all Notes on the line with the Treble Clef, are called G, and all Notes on the line with the Base Clef, are called F.

Give Examples according to the following Clefs.

What is the difference between a Chromatic and a Diatonic Semitone?

A Chromatic Semitone remains on the same degree of the

Staff, and is called by the same letter, as 

whereas a Diatonic Semitone changes its degrees and name, thus: 

What is the meaning of Enharmonic?

The Enharmonic Diesis, or Quarter Tone, is the difference between two following Notes, one of which is raised, and the other lowered a Chromatic Semitone. This Interval cannot be expressed on the Piano-Forte, from its construction; but the same Keys must be struck for the Sharp of the lowest Note, and the Flat of the highest.

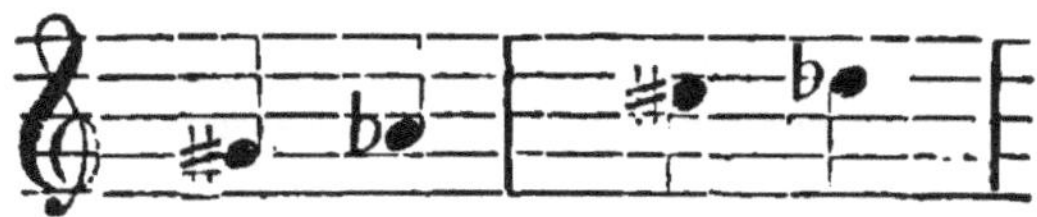

CHAPTER XII.

EXPLANATION OF MUSICAL TERMS.

A, signifies in, for, at, with, &c.
Adagio, a slow movement.
Ad Libitum, or *Ad Lib.*, at pleasure.
Affetuoso, in a style of execution adapted to express affection, tenderness, and deep emotion.
Air, the leading part or melody.
Allegro, a brisk and sprightly movement.
Allegretto, less quick then Allegro.
Allegro, ma non troppo, brisk, but not too fast.
Alto, the Counter Tenor part, or that between the Tenor and Treble.
Amoroso, in a soft and delicate style.
Andante moderately slow.
Andantino, quicker than Andante.
Animato, or *Con Anima*, with animation.

Anthem, a portion of Scripture, set to music.

Assai, more. Generally used with some other word to denote an increase or diminution of the time.

Barytone, a voice whose register is between the Base and the Tenor.

Base, the lowest part in harmony.

Bis, twice. This term denotes a repetition of a passage in music.

Brillante, in a gay and lively manner.

Cadence, repose; the termination of a Harmonical phrase on a repose, or on a perfect chord.

Calando, a diminution of time and sound, till the sound is nearly lost to the ear.

Canon, a kind of perpetual fugue, in which the different parts, beginning one after another, repeat incessantly the same Airs.

Cantabile, an elegant, smooth, graceful style.

Canto, a song. It signifies also the Treble part or Air.

Canto Fermo, plain song.

Chant, a peculiar kind of sacred music, in which prose is sung with less variety of intonation than in common airs.

Chord, the combination of two or more sounds uttered at the same time, according to the laws of harmony; as a third, fifth, and eighth, which are perfect Chords. The fourth, and sixth, are imperfect chords.

Chorus, a composition or passage, designed for all the voices and instruments.

Chromatic, a term given to accidental semitones.

Coda, the close of a composition, or an additional close.

Con, with, as *Con Spirito*, with spirit. *Con Brio*, with life.

Con furia, with boldness.

Cusando, with an increasing volume of sound.

Contralto, the lowest female voice.

Crescendo, or *Cres.*, or $<$, with an increasing volume of sound.

Da Capo, or *D. C.*, close with the first strain.

Del, by. *Del Segno*, repeat from the sign.

Diapason, the Octavo or Interval which excludes all the tones.

Diminuendo, or *Dim.*, or $>$, with a decreasing volume.

Dirge, a piece composed for Funeral occasions.

Divoto, in a solemn and devout manner.

Dolce, sweet and soft.

Doloroso, pathetic.

Dominant, the fifth Note above the Tonic.
Duetto, or *Duett*, music consisting of two parts.
E, and, as *Moderato e Pianissimo*.
Expression, that union of qualities in a composition, from which we derive a sentimental appeal to our feelings.
Expressivo, with expression.
Enharmonic Modulations, sounds, which are identical in pitch, but placed on different degrees, are called *enharmonic*.
Fagotto, the Bassoon part.
Fine, the end of a piece.
Forte, or *For.*, or *F.*, or *f.*, strong and full.
Fortissimo, or *FF.*, or *ff.*, very loud.
Forzando, or *fz.*, the notes over which this term is placed, are to be boldly struck and continued.
Fugue, or *Fuge*, a piece in which one of the parts leads, and the rest follow in different intervals of time, and in the same or similar melody.
Grave, or *Gravemente*, slow and solemn.
Grazioso, graceful; a smoth and gentle style of execution, approaching to Piano.
Guisto, in equal, steady, just time.
Harmony, an agreable combination of musical sounds, or different melodies, performed at the same time.
Interlude, an instrumental passage introduced between two vocal passages.
Interval, a musical sound. Also the distance between any two sounds, either in harmony or melody.
Largo, a slow movement. A quaver in Largo equals a minim in Presto.
Larghetto, quicker than Largo.
Legato, signifies that the notes of the passage are to be performed in a close, smoth, aud gliding manner.
Lentando, or *Lent*, gradually retarding the time.
Lento,
Lentemente, } slow, smooth and gliding.
Ma, not.
Ma non Troppo, not too much, not in excess.
Maestoso, with grandeur of expression.
Melody, an agreeable succession of sounds.
Metronome, an instrument, which, by a short pendulum with a sliding weight, and set in motion by clock-work, serves to measure time in Music.
Mezza Voce, with a medium fullness of tone.
Mezzo, half, middle, mean.

Moderato, between Andante and Allegro.
Motto, much.
Motet, a musical composition of a sacred character, consisting of from one to eight parts.
Non, not.
Non troppo presto, not too qnick.
Oratorio, a species of Musical Drama, consisting of airs, recitatives, duetts, trios, choruses &c.
Orchestra, the place or band of *secular* musical performances.
Overture, in dramatic music, is an instrumental strain, which serves as an introduction.
Pastorale, in a rural or pastorale style.
Piano, or *Pia.*, or *P.*, or *p.*, soft.
Pianissimo, or *P P.*, or *pp.*, very soft.
Piu, prefixed to another word increases its force.
Pizzicato, snapping the violin strings instead of employing the bow.
Poco, little, somewhat.
Pomposo, grand and dignified.
Presto, quick.
Prestissimo, very quick.
Primo, the first or leading part.
Quartetto, a composition consisting of four parts, each of which occasionally takes the leading melody.
Quintetto, Music composed in five parts, each of which occasionally takes the leading melody.
Recitative, a sort of style resembling speaking.
Ripieno, applied to such parts as are intended to fill up the chorus.
Ritornello, a short intermediate symphony.
Secondo, the second part.
Semi-Chorus, half the choir of voices.
Sempre, throughout; as, *Sempre Piano*, soft throughout.
Semplice, chaste and simple.
Senza, without; as, *Senza Organo*, without the organ.
Siciliano, a slow, graceful movement in compound time.
Soave, agreeable, pleasing.
Solfeggio, the system of arranging the Scales by the names Do, Re, Mi, Fa, Sol, La, Si, by which singing is taught.
Soli, plural of *Solo*, but denoting only one voice to each of the several parts.
Solo, a composition designed for a single voice or instrument. Vocal solos, duetts, &c., in modern music, are usually accompanied with instruments.

Soprano, the Treble, or higher voice part.
Sostenuto, sustaining the sounds to the uttermost of their nominal value in time.
Sotto Voce, middling strength of voice.
Spiritoso, with spirit.
Staccato, the opposite to Legato; requiring a short, articulate, and distinct style of performance.
Sub-Dominant, the fourth Note above the Tonic, or the fifth below the Tonic.
Subito, quick.
Symphony or *Sym.*, a passage to be executed by instruments, while the vocal performers are silent. Also a species of musical composition.
Tardo, slowly.
Tasto Solo or *T. S.*, denotes that the passage should be performed with no other chords than unisons and octaves.
Tacit, be silent.
Tempo, time; as *A Tempo*, or *Tempo Giusto*, in true time.
Tempo di Marcia, Martial time.
Ten, *Tenuto*, sustained after the style of Legato.
Tenor, high male voice.
Thorough Base, the instrumental Base, with figures for the Organ.
Treble, the female voice.
Trio, a composition for three voices.
Tutti, all together.
Veloce, quick.
Verse, one voice to a part.
Vigoroso, with energy.
Vivace, in a brisk and lively manner
Volti, turn over.
Voce di Tetto, the head voice.
Voce di Petto, the chest voice.

CONTENTS.

CHAPTER I.
Of the Keys, Staff, &c. - - - - 5

CHAPTER II.
Of the Length of Notes, Rests, &c. - - 8

CHAPTER III.
Of Time, - - - - - - 14

CHAPTER IV.
Of the Position of the Hand, and manner of Playing, 17

CHAPTER V.
Of Sharps, Flats, &c. - - - - 24

CHAPTER VI.
Of Common Characters used in Music, - - 27

CHAPTER VII.
Of Graces, and Common Marks of Expression, - 30

CHAPTER VIII.
Of Intervals, - - - - - - 33

CHAPTER IX.
Of the Signature, - - - - - 34

CHAPTER X.
Of the Formation of the Scale, - - - 37

CHAPTER XI.
Of the various Characters used in Music, - - 40

CHAPTER XII.
Explanation of Musical Terms, - - - 45

www.ingramcontent.com/pod-product-compliance
Lightning Source LLC
Chambersburg PA
CBHW032120080426
42733CB00008B/1000

9783744793506